Looping with
DISNEY · PIXAR
FINDING DORY

Allyssa Loya

Lerner Publications ◆ Minneapolis

Lerner Publications Company
A division of Lerner Publishing Group, Inc.
241 First Avenue North
Minneapolis, MN 55401 USA

For reading levels and more information, look up this title at www.lernerbooks.com.

Additional graphics provided by Laura Westlund/Independent Picture Service.

Main body text set in Billy Infant Regular 14/20.
Typeface provided by SparkyType.

Library of Congress Cataloging-in-Publication Data

Names: Loya, Allyssa, author.
Title: Looping with Finding Dory / Allyssa Loya.
Description: Minneapolis, MN : Lerner Publications Company, [2018] | Series: Disney
    coding adventures | Includes bibliographical references and index. | Audience: Ages
    6-9. | Audience: Grades K to 3.
Identifiers: LCCN 2018001212 (print) | LCCN 2018006019 (ebook) |
    ISBN 9781541524330 (eb pdf) | ISBN 9781541524293 (lb : alk. paper) |
    ISBN 9781541526761 (pb : alk. paper)
Subjects: LCSH: Loop tiling (Computer science)—Juvenile literature. | Finding Dory
    (Motion picture)—Juvenile literature.
Classification: LCC QA76.52 (ebook) | LCC QA76.52 .L69 2018 (print) | DDC 005.4/53—
    dc23

LC record available at https://lccn.loc.gov/2018001212

Manufactured in the United States of America
1-44517-34767-4/13/2018

Table of Contents

What Is Looping?. 4

Have You Seen My Parents? 6

Get to the Jewel of Morro Bay! 8

Keep Gerald off the Rocks 12

Help Us, Becky! Ooo-Roo! 14

Guide Hank to the Open Ocean Exhibit . . 16

The Touch Pool 18

Destiny. 20

Echolocation 22

Escaping the Pipes. 24

Follow the Shells 26

Keep Coding! 28

Answer Key 30
Glossary 30
Further Information 31
Index 32

What Is Looping?

How do video game characters know what to do? The instructions that tell them to kick or jump are code. Think of each line of code as a step. An algorithm is a series of steps, or a set of instructions.

Sometimes algorithms include the same lines of code many times in a row. Algorithms use loops to repeat these steps easily. A loop tells a computer how many times to do the same thing.

An algorithm without a loop may look like this: ↓ ↓ ↓ ↓
The same algorithm with a loop looks like this: 4 (↓)

Both examples tell the computer to move down four times. The algorithm with a loop is easier to write. It tells the computer to do the action inside the parentheses four times.

Looping can help solve problems just like the ones Dory and her friends face in *Finding Dory*. For some of these projects, you'll need a partner, plain paper, construction paper, a stuffed toy, scissors, pencils, and crayons.

Have You Seen My Parents?

Dory lost her family. She asks the fish nearby if they've seen her parents. Your partner will pretend to be Dory. Then you can guide Dory to different fish to ask for help.

Cut four squares of paper, and draw fish on them. Put them in different places around the room. Then tell your partner what steps to take to reach each fish. Think of each step as a line of code. Anything your partner will do more than once is a loop. For example, the steps might be: take 3 steps left, take 3 steps forward.

Keep going until your partner
reaches all the fish.

Get to the Jewel of Morro Bay!

Dory remembers where to find her family! She must swim to the Jewel of Morro Bay.

Look at the paths on the next three pages. Then decompose them. That means to think about each step in the path. For each path, choose the looped line of code that will get Dory to her goal.

Swim to the Turtles

Dory needs to catch a ride to find her parents. Choose the answer from the list below that will help her get to the turtle.

A 5(→)

B 3(↑)

C 5(↓)

Check your answers on page 30.

START

9

Ride the Current

Far out, dude! Dory found the turtles, and they're ready to go. Which looped algorithm below will help them ride the current?

A 2(⬇) 9(➡) 4(⬇)

B 3(⬆) 9(⬅) 3(⬇)

C 2(⬇) 5(➡) 6(⬇)

START

END

Escape the Squid

Dory is almost there! Choose the looped algorithm from the list below that will help her finish her journey to Morro Bay.

A 4(⬇) 8(⬅) 3(⬆) 6(➡) 2(➡)

B 2(⬇) 8(⬅) 3(⬇) 8(➡) 2(⬇)

C 3(⬅) 3(⬇) 2(⬆) 8(➡) 4(⬇)

START

ESCAPE

Keep Gerald off the Rocks

Fluke and Rudder love their rock. They want to keep Gerald off, off, off! They always move toward him and bark when he tries to get on.

Look at the map on page 12. How would you keep Gerald off the rock? Maybe you would move Fluke and Rudder across the rock. Then you could add a line to bark when they reach Gerald. In that case, an algorithm for the map on page 12 might be:

3 (➡) Bark!

This algorithm tells Fluke and Rudder to move right three times and then bark at Gerald.

Use looped lines of code to write an algorithm for the map on this page.

Help Us, Becky! Ooo-Roo!

Nemo and Marlin need help getting to Quarantine. Becky is there to help. Or is she?

Grab a partner and two stuffed toys. The stuffed toys will be Nemo and Marlin. Look around the room, and choose a start point and an end point. The start and end points can be anywhere in the room. On your own paper, write an algorithm with looped lines of code to show Becky how to get to the end. It doesn't have to be a straight line. For example, your algorithm could look like this:

3(⬆) 2(➡) 4(⬆) 2 (➡)

The steps you choose depend on your path through the room.

Your partner will pretend to be Becky and carry the stuffed animals. If your partner follows the algorithm and it doesn't work, that means it has a bug, or mistake. You need to resolve, or fix, it. Rewrite the algorithm until it can run with no bugs. That means your partner can follow the instructions and make it to the end.

Guide Hank to the Open Ocean Exhibit

Hank is using a stroller to take Dory to the *Open Ocean* exhibit. He can't see out of the stroller, so Hank has to follow Dory's instructions. Dory should think carefully about each step in the path.

Pretend that you are Dory, giving Hank directions to the *Open Ocean* exhibit. Look at the map on the next page. Then plan each step to guide Hank. Write an algorithm on your own paper that uses loops to get Hank to the exhibit. Watch out for people and objects in your way. When you're done, run your algorithm to see if it works. If there is a bug, resolve it and try again.

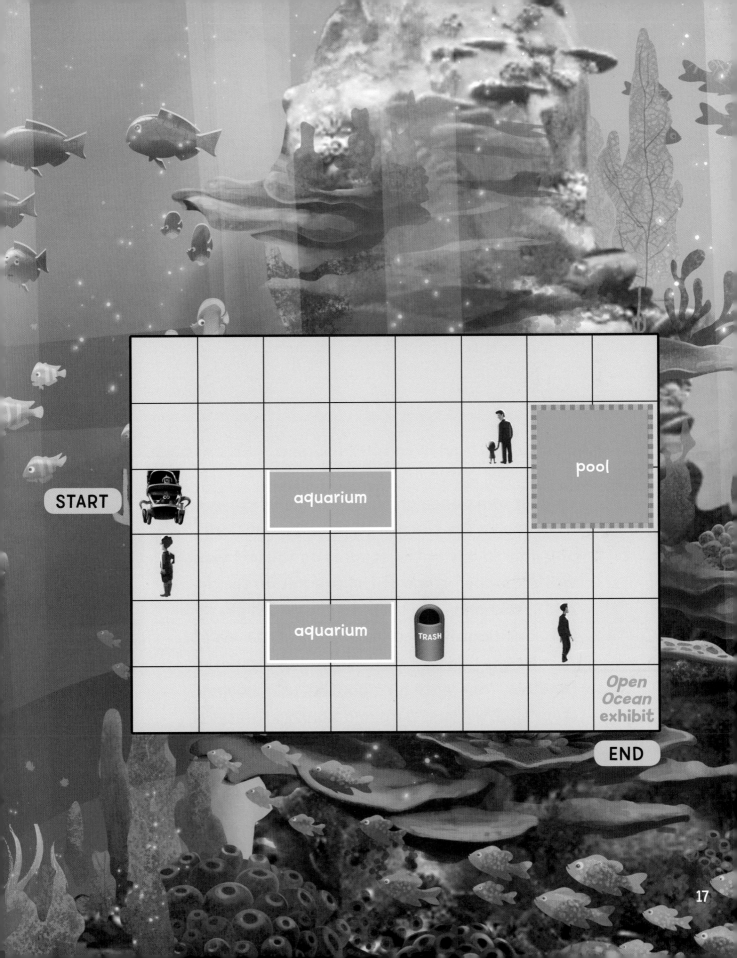

START

aquarium

pool

aquarium

TRASH

Open
Ocean
exhibit

END

The Touch Pool

Oh no! Dory and Hank are trapped in the touch pool! Help them escape.

On your own paper, draw a grid with five rows and five columns like the one on page 19. Put Dory and Hank in one of the squares on the left side. Write "Escape" in one of the squares on the right. Add some hands and rocks to the grid. Make sure Dory and Hank have at least one path to escape.

Show the grid to a partner, and decompose it together. Then write an algorithm using looped steps that will lead Dory and Hank to safety.

Destiny

Destiny wants to help Dory, but the whale shark can't see clearly. Luckily, Bailey the beluga is there to guide Destiny.

You already know how to loop one line of code. Looping doesn't stop there! You can loop multiple lines of code too. For example, say you wanted to move in a square. You could write an algorithm like this: 4(⬆, turn right).

That algorithm tells you to step forward and then turn right. The number says to repeat each step in order four times. You walked in a square!

Pretend you're Bailey and a partner is Destiny. Look at the room around you. Then choose a path through the room. Write an algorithm to follow the path that loops multiple lines of code. Then have your partner run the algorithm by following the instructions. Did it work the way you wanted? Try different paths and algorithms with steps such as sit, stand, and jump.

Echolocation

Bailey has a very cool power. His echolocation uses sound to let him sense things he can't even see. Bailey uses this ability to imagine a map of the pipes below the Marine Life Institute.

Look at the pipe on this page. Then write an algorithm to guide Dory through the pipe. Use a loop with multiple lines of code. Run the algorithm when it's finished. Did Dory make it to the end? If not, the algorithm has a bug. Resolve it and try again.

START

END

Escaping the Pipes

Dory is still lost in the pipes. But with Destiny shouting directions, Dory is sure to escape.

When Dory swims to a place where two pipes meet, she must listen for Destiny's directions. Look at the map on the next page. Then look at the lines of code above it. On your own paper, arrange the lines of code into an algorithm that will help Dory escape. Remember, Dory cannot swim through rocks.

Follow the Shells

Make a line of shells that will lead Dory to her family!

In this activity, you will use a do-until loop. A do-until loop keeps going until something happens. Then the loop stops. For example, a do-until loop for Dory might be this: do until you find your parents (swim, search).

Cut a sheet of construction paper into ten pieces. Draw a shell on three of the pieces. Draw Dory's parents on one of the pieces. Then draw rocks on the rest.

Place the rocks on the floor around the room. Put the three shells in a line. Then place Dory's parents at the end of the line.

Ask your partner to be Dory. Your partner will use this do-until loop to search for the shells: do until you find the line of shells (swim, ignore rocks).

Once Dory has found the line of shells, your partner will use this do-until loop to find Dory's parents: do until you find your parents (follow the line of shells, swim).

Keep Coding!

You know that algorithms are just sets of clear instructions. You also know a lot about loops. Think about the steps you repeat during your day.

You repeat steps when you brush your teeth. Tell yourself how many times to loop the brush across your teeth. See if that gets them clean!

When you're walking to the door, guess how many steps it will take to get there. Think about a looped line of code. Then see if you're right.

Look at your food during lunch. How many bites will it take to eat? How many times will you chew each bite?

You can even think about do-until loops during the day. For example,

- do until school is over (listen, learn)
- do until the food is ready to be swallowed (chew)

You can find lots of chances to think about looping!

Answer Key

Page 9: A

Page 10: A

Page 11: B

Page 13: 3(➡) 3(⬆) Bark! (*possible answer*)

Page 17: ➡⬇6(➡) 2(⬇) (*possible answer*)

Page 23: 3(2⬇, 3➡)

Page 25: 3(➡) listen 3(⬆) listen 4(➡) listen 3(⬇) listen 3(➡) listen 2(➡)

Glossary

algorithm: a group of instructions, made up of lines of code, that tells your computer how to solve a problem or finish a job

bug: a mistake found in lines of code

code: instructions written for computers to follow

decompose: to take a big problem and break it down into small pieces to figure it out

do-until loop: a loop that continues until a condition is met

loop: a line of code that tells a computer to repeat one or more instructions a certain number of times

resolve: fix

run: to start an algorithm

Further Information

CodeMonkey
https://www.playcodemonkey.com

Code.org
https://code.org/learn

Kelly, James F. *The Story of Coding*. New York: DK, 2017.

Lyons, Heather. *Coding in the Real World*. Minneapolis: Lerner Publications, 2018.

Matteson, Adrienne. *Coding with ScratchJr.* Ann Arbor, MI: Cherry Lake, 2017.

Index

bug, 15–16, 23

code, 4, 6, 8, 13–14, 20-21, 23–24, 28

computer, 4

decompose, 8, 18

resolve, 15–16, 23

About the Author

Allyssa Loya is an elementary school librarian in North Texas. Her passion for bringing meaningful learning to students led her to cultivate a technology-forward library that includes a makerspace and a coding club. While running the coding club in the library, she realized how important it is for every student to experience coding. Not every student will grow up to be a computer programmer, but all students will need to know how to think clearly and critically when they are adults.

Loya is married to an IT manager, who is a perfect support system for her technological endeavors. Her two young boys are a constant reminder of the experiences that all students deserve from their educators.